modern readers — stage 4

What if...?

Liani Moraes

© LIANI MORAES, 2005

Richmond

Diretoria: *Paul Berry*
Gerência editorial: *Sandra Possas*
Coordenação de revisão: *Estevam Vieira Lédo Jr.*
Coordenação de produção gráfica: *André Monteiro, Maria de Lourdes Rodrigues*
Coordenação de produção industrial: *Wilson Troque*

Projeto editorial: *Kylie Mackin*

Edição e preparação de texto: *Kylie Mackin*
Assistência editorial: *Gabriela Peixoto Vilanova*
Revisão: *Fernanda Marcelino*
Projeto gráfico de miolo e capa: *Ricardo Van Steen Comunicações e Propaganda Ltda./Oliver Fuchs*
Edição de arte: *Christiane Borin*
Ilustrações de miolo e capa: *Cris Eich e Jean-Claude*
Diagramação: *Formato Comunicação*
Pré-impressão: *Helio P. de Souza Filho, Marcio H. Kamoto*
Impressão e acabamento: *Digital Page gráfica e editora*

Dados Internacionais de Catalogação na Publicação (CIP)
(Câmara Brasileira do Livro, SP, Brasil)

Moraes, Liani
    What if...? / Liani Moraes ; ilustração Cris Eich e Jean-Claude. — São Paulo : Richmond Publishing, 2004. —
(Modern readers ; stage 4)

    1. Inglês (Ensino fundamental) I. Eich, Cris. II. Jean-Claude. III. Título. IV. Série.

04-2412   CDD-372.652

Índices para catálogo sistemático:
1. Inglês : Ensino fundamental   372.652

ISBN 85-16-04155-7

Reprodução proibida. Art. 184 do Código Penal e Lei 9.610 de 19 de fevereiro de 1998.

Todos os direitos reservados.

RICHMOND
EDITORA MODERNA LTDA.
Rua Padre Adelino, 758 — Belenzinho
São Paulo — SP — Brasil — CEP 03303-904
Central de atendimento ao usuário: 0800 771 8181
www.richmond.com.br
2014

Impresso no Brasil

This is no ordinary story. Actually, it's the story of a special girl I knew some years ago. During my career as a Biology teacher, I've tried to help many girls like the one I'm going to tell you about.

Barbara was a shy girl. But every night, she used to meet her five e-friends in their private chat room. The girls were Julia, Sofia, Lisa and Carol. Her web pals used to call Barbara by her nickname, Babs.

Julia, Sofia and Lisa studied at the same school and did lots of things together. Barbara lived in another neighborhood and attended another school.

The fifth net friend, Carol, lived in Buenos Aires.

Only Julia had met her in person during a camping trip to Argentina. They were all in their second year of senior high school when everything happened.

The friends had many things in common. Their favorite pastimes were reading teen magazines, going to shopping malls, and of course, chatting online. For more than a year, they had shared their dreams and anxieties. They had talked about boys, fashionable clothes, interesting movies, magazines, parties, music, and sometimes, about school, too. They had exchanged photos via internet and this made them even closer. Only Lisa and Barbara had steady boyfriends.

Julia: Hi, guys! Are you all there?
Lisa: Sure, girls. What's new?
Carol: Bad weather here in Buenos Aires — rainy and windy.
Barbara: My turn now, girls. I'm in love with Eric. The problem is that my mom isn't so happy about it. She says I'm too young to date, especially a boy eight years older than me. But I love him, I love him, I love him! What can I do?
Carol: Be yourself and keep on dating. We are A and B students. We deserve a little fun, don't we?
Lisa: Tom and I have been together for about six months now. My mother thinks it's OK, but my father complains a lot because he is only a year older than I am.

Julia: Parents are never happy with what we do. Boyfriends are either too old, or too young, too short or too tall, talk too much or are too quiet. Who can please parents? I have given up trying.

Barbara: Our parents have the right to worry about us. It's their way of saying *'I love you'*. But we have to live our own lives!

Julia: Lucky me that I'm not interested in anybody right now.

Lisa: I can't believe you aren't interested in anyone, Julia.

Julia: It's true, guys. After Mr Muscles and I broke up, I sealed my heart for good. I'm not saying it's forever, of course. I just want a break.

Lisa: Bed time, babies!

Barbara: Bye, everyone. I'm going to dream about Eric, the one and only.

The following night, in the chat room...

Lisa: Hello, girls! What do you think about that advice section in **Just for Teens**, the one signed by Dr Doris Devane? Do you think she's a real psychologist?

Sofia: Are you looking for advice?

Lisa: It's kind of secret, but I can trust you guys. My boyfriend says we should have sex. We have already come close to it, but I'm not sure. If I do, there's no turning back. What do you think, girls?

Carol: I don't know. Having a steady boyfriend doesn't mean you are going to be together forever. On the other hand, lots of girls do it. I think it's no big deal. I don't have enough experience to tell you what to do, but why don't you write to Dr Devane?

Barbara: Maybe I'll write, too. Eric is also kind of insisting that we should make love soon. After all, we've been together for almost six months now.

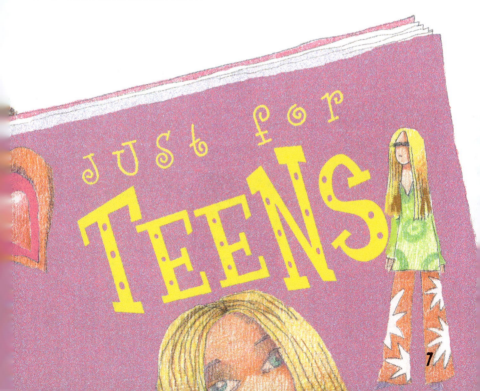

Julia: There are better people to get advice from, guys. How can you trust a magazine psychologist when you don't even know if she's a real shrink?

Sofia: I believe our favorite magazine is serious. They wouldn't fake a thing like this.

Carol: One thing is for sure though. Lots of people write to magazines. Lisa could write and if her letter is published, at least we'll know it's real. What do you think, Lisa?

Lisa: I'll think about it. Oh, another thing! Have you done your homework?

Julia: Which homework?

Lisa: The questionnaire. Susan, our Biology teacher, says she needs more information about what teenagers know about sexuality and Sexually Transmitted Diseases.

Sofia: I remember now. Let's go so we have time to fill it in.

QUESTIONNAIRE

This questionnaire is strictly confidential. Imagine you are the main subject in all the situations hypothetically described below:

1) What's the importance of wearing a condom during intercourse?

2) If you are a boy, do you know the right way to put on a condom so that it can really protect you?

3) You and your boyfriend/girlfriend have been dating steadily for over a year. You decide to start having sexual relations. What should you do before you start?

4) Do you believe you are well-informed about how to avoid pregnancy and STD's (Sexually Transmitted Diseases)?

5) Do you talk to your family about these issues? Do they provide you with information about them?

6) Are your friends and teen magazines your only source of information about sex?

7) Do you access the internet to get additional information about sex? Which sites?

8) What are your main doubts in regards to sex?

9) Do you think your school is a good place to get information about sex?

10) Would you feel free to talk about sex in front of your classmates?

After a few days...

Lisa: Girls, I've finally decided to write Dr Doris a letter asking about you know what.

Julia: She's not going to say: **Do it**, or **Don't do it**. I'm sure she will advise you about the use of contraceptives if you have sex.

Barbara: My boyfriend says that sex with a condom is no good.

Julia: But it's safe, Babs. What if you get pregnant?

Barbara: He says he knows a way to avoid pregnancy.

Sofia: Don't be so sure about it. Maybe he's just trying to make you do something you don't really want to do.

Barbara: Who says I don't want to?

Sofia: You should think about whether you are really ready to have sex or not. After all, you haven't been dating long.

Lisa: I know it's a big decision, but I think Tom and I will do it really soon. That's what we both want. He says he'll wear a condom. We don't want to take any chances.

Carol: Are you going to tell your mom?

Lisa: No way! Of course not! She would crucify me.

Barbara: I wouldn't tell mine either. I think it's a private matter.

April 12

Dear Diary

Sometimes I feel so insecure... I don't know what to do. Eric has invited me to go to his parents' beach house. We would tell our parents we were going to a friend's house with a group. He says he will call my mother to ask permission. I know that if we go, we'll make love and I'm not so sure I want to. My web friends are the only ones I can open my heart to. My brother is too distant, and my mother is too busy to worry about me. My dad lives far away from us. Besides, he has another family now. When I get married, it'll be forever. (Wow! It sounds like a song). My children won't go through what my brother and I did when our parents split. I'm sleepy now. It's not a good time t[o] make any big decisions. I'll call Eric tomorrow. can't wait to hear his voice.

12

Lisa came home from school and decided to write Dr Doris Devane a letter.

Dear Doris

I'm sixteen years old. I have a boyfriend who is really cute. He is a year older than I am. We love each other. Tom is such a nice guy. He asked me to have sex with him. I can't talk to my mom about it. My friends and I share a private chat room and we talk every night. The problem is they don't feel secure enough to offer me any advice. Please, help me. Should I sleep with him or not? Am I too young? I feel like an adult and so does he.

My friends and I had a discussion about you the other day. We were wondering if you really exist. Are you a creation of the magazine and some journalist answers the letters from the readers?

Lisa

Three weeks later, Lisa's letter was finally published in Dr Devane's advice column, **Just Ask Doris**. The girls were very excited to see their friend's letter in their favorite magazine.

Dr. Devan
ADVICE COLUMN

Dear Lisa

Being in love is not enough to decide if you are going to have sex with your boyfriend or not, especially because you are only sixteen. Talk to an older person you can trust. Your mother or an older sister would be best. If you really want to start a sex life, go to a doctor first. You must be aware of the risk of getting pregnant and you also have to know about STD's and how to avoid them. Good luck.

PS: I'm a real psychologist, not a fake.

In the chat room...

Barbara: I feel Eric is kind of compelling me to sleep with him.

Julia: You don't have to do it. The decision is up to you.

Barbara: I'm afraid he'll leave me if I don't.

Julia: C'mon, girl! If you sleep with him, do it because you want to, not to please him or just because you're afraid of losing him.

Carol: Julia's right, Babs. Think about it.

One day, about a month and a half later, Barbara didn't show up in the chat room as usual. And she didn't come in the day after that, or the next. The four girls were worried. They didn't have her phone number so they couldn't call her up and find out what had happened.

They were beginning to lose hope when, one day, Sofia read a letter addressed to Dr Doris in the advice column of **Just for Teens**. The girl signed the letter as Babs.

Dear Doris

I'm in big trouble. My boyfriend and I have been together for about eight months. We made love for the first time two months ago. He insisted a lot and I finally gave in. I was afraid of losing him if I didn't agree. He told me that if we had sexual relations just before my period, I wouldn't get pregnant. But I did. Now I'm expecting a baby and I don't know what to do. I feel miserable. I haven't told my mom and my best friends yet. I feel like I'm all alone.

My boyfriend says I should have an abortion, but I think it's wrong. I would feel guilty for the rest of my life and I don't want to do anything illegal. I know I was careless (we both were), but I'm only 16. We imagine these things only happen to other people. I've always tried to do the right thing. I'm a good student and I've never used drugs. And now, my world has collapsed. What should I do? Please, help me.

Babs

Sofia read the letter again and again and finally decided to call Julia up. "Sofia, it has to be her," — Julia said. It's too much of a coincidence that she has disappeared and now a girl with the same name writes to a magazine asking for advice."

"And she sure is in big trouble. What can we do?" — Sofia asked anxiously.

"What do you think if...?" — Julia replied.

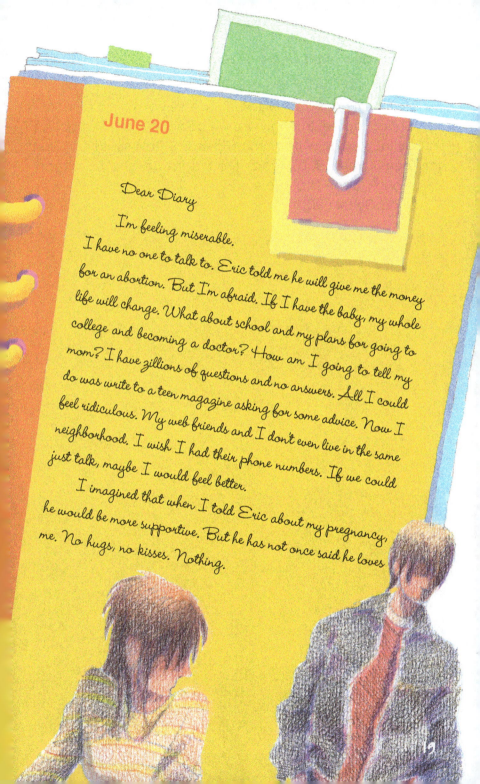

June 20

Dear Diary

I'm feeling miserable.

I have no one to talk to. Eric told me he will give me the money for an abortion. But I'm afraid. If I have the baby, my whole life will change. What about school and my plans for going to college and becoming a doctor? How am I going to tell my mom? I have zillions of questions and no answers. All I could do was write to a teen magazine asking for some advice. Now I feel ridiculous. My web friends and I don't even live in the same neighborhood. I wish I had their phone numbers. If we could just talk, maybe I would feel better.

I imagined that when I told Eric about my pregnancy, he would be more supportive. But he has not once said he loves me. No hugs, no kisses. Nothing.

That same night, in the chat room...

Carol: Your idea is great, Julia.
Julia: I'm not sure it will work, but we can give it a shot.
Sofia: I agree. But how are we going to make contact?
Julia: We can write to that **Friends & Pals** section of **Just for Teens**. When Babs reads the magazine, she'll probably come back to the chat room.
Julia: So let's do it!

Friends & Pals

Dear Babs

We are your old friends: Julia, Sofia, Lisa and Carol. We are really worried about you and we want to help. We will be waiting for you at the same time and place. Don't let us down. We miss you.

Your four e-friends

That night, Eric met Igor, his best friend, at their local bar. Eric seemed depressed. Igor was trying to comfort him.

"Hey, man! What's up?"

"I think I've messed up, brother. My girlfriend is pregnant. I don't know what to do."

"What about an abortion? Don't you think you are too young to be a father? How old is she?"

"Only sixteen. That's the problem. Just imagine what will happen when she tells her family? When I mentioned an abortion, she got upset. She said she can't even think about such a thing. I'm lost, man."

"Do your parents know?"

"Not yet. I'll have to face them, and her mother too. Her parents are divorced and I don't even know her father because he lives in another state. I feel ashamed and responsible. You're right. The truth is we are both too young to be parents. I'm eight years older than she is, but I haven't finished college yet and I'm just not prepared to be a father. It's my fault. I insisted that she have sex and I was careless," — Eric sighed.

"C'mon, man! It isn't the end of the world. You're not the first one this has happened to. Things will work out OK."

"I feel guilty because she is just a kid."

"I'll be here for you, brother." — Igor added. "And try to convince her to have an abortion. She's too young to be a mother. I think even her mom will agree with that. Cheer up, man! After all, you are not the only one to blame."

After class, the girls rushed to Julia's house to read the new issue of **Just for Teens** magazine. Their letter was there! They could hardly believe it.

"What if she doesn't read the letter? What if she doesn't come to the chat room tonight?" — asked Sofia anxiously.

"No more **what if's**, Sofia," — Julia replied seriously. "Let's just wait.

The two following nights, the girls waited for their friend, but she didn't show up.

Three days later...

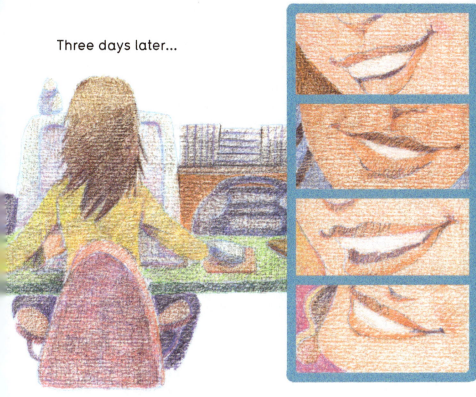

Barbara: Hi guys! I've missed you so much! I feel so ashamed. I'm so sorry, girls...

Julia: Hey, don't apologize Babs. We're just happy that you're back! You didn't do anything wrong. You were careless, that's all.

Barbara: You make things seem easy, Julia. But they're not, at least for me.

Julia: I know they aren't. But we are here to help you.

Sofia: We just couldn't believe it when we read your letter in the magazine! We were sure it was you. You are in our hearts and minds every day. And you have our total support, no matter what.

Barbara: Stop, girls. I'm starting to cry. Oh, my God, I missed you so much! I'm sorry I disappointed you.

Julia: Please, Babs. Stop hurting yourself. You didn't let us down. But don't ever think of leaving again, kiddo. Have you talked to your family yet?

25

Barbara: Yes. My mom was very supportive. I didn't expect that. And my father is coming home next week to visit us. He's really worried. My brother didn't talk to me for a week, but then he came to my room and apologized. We hugged and for the first time in my life I feel I have a family who really cares about me. My father hasn't even blamed my mom for what happened.

Carol: Are you going to school?

Barbara: Yes. In the beginning I wanted to quit. But my mom told me I had to face it. My school coordinator has also talked to me. And the teachers have been very supportive as well. They said I have nothing to be ashamed of.

Lisa: What about the baby?

Barbara: I still have to think about it. I'm afraid of having an abortion. But I don't want to give up my plans for going to college.

Julia: What about Eric?

Barbara: Well, I feel he's changed a lot. Sometimes he hugs and kisses me, but it's not the same thing. Next year he is traveling abroad on a scholarship. I'm not sure we'll stay together after all.

Lisa: Just live one day at a time, Babs, and trust your feelings.

Barbara: My dad doesn't think I should have an abortion. He told me he'll help me raise my baby. My mom agrees with him.

Carol: What about Eric's parents?

Barbara: His father is in favor of an abortion. He says he'll pay for it. His mom says it's up to me to decide. In the beginning, Eric wanted me to have an abortion, too. Now he's not so sure. He told me it's my decision, and nobody else's.

Sofia: My mom is a doctor, you know. She's a gynecologist. If you want, I'll make an appointment for you.

Barbara: I think it's a good idea. I'll talk to my mom and ask her to go with me.

July 2

Dear Diary

Some nights I can't get to sleep easily. I keep thinking about myself, my family, Eric, and the baby. Why me? The first time I made love, I got pregnant. It's not fair! Tomorrow my dad will be here. In a certain way, I also feel happy. My mom and I are closer now and my brother is being very nice, too. Not to mention my e-friends, my teachers, my school coordinator and many of my classmates. Eric and I were not prepared for what happened. Why didn't he wear a condom? The first time wasn't what I had expected. It was romantic but I just didn't feel that much pleasure. Now I'm sick all the time. I'll have to stop writing because I think I'm going to throw up again.

Barbara and her mother were in the waiting room of Dr Beatriz Martin's office. Babs was nervous. The day before, she told her mother that she wanted to talk to Dr Martin alone. She would ask the doctor to call her at the end of the appointment. Her belly still wasn't showing but she felt as if everybody was staring at her. It was as if the word **pregnant** was written in big letters on her forehead. She tried to pay attention to the magazine she had got from a side table, but she just couldn't. When she heard her name she stood up fast and went in.

Dr Martin was very understanding. She kissed and hugged Barbara as she went in. The doctor was younger than she had imagined, and very attractive. She began: "Well, doctor, you know why I'm here."

"Yes, Barbara, but I want to hear it from you. How are things?"

As she started talking, and looking at Dr Martin's friendly smile, she felt her fears were beginning to melt away. As she spoke the doctor asked questions and took notes. At the end of the appointment, the doctor said: "You know, Barbara, what happened to you is not that unusual. If you want, I'll help you during your pregnancy so that you can have a healthy baby. Early pregnancy implies some risks for both the mother and the baby. It's my duty to keep those risks to a minimum. Feel free to ask me anything. You will also need psychological counseling so I'm going to recommend you to a good psychologist."

When Barbara told Dr Martin she was in doubt about having the baby or not, the doctor replied: "If you decide not to have the baby, I can't help you with that. It's unethical for me to recommend somebody to perform an abortion. I don't do it and neither do my colleagues. It's only done under very special circumstances. Otherwise, it's illegal."

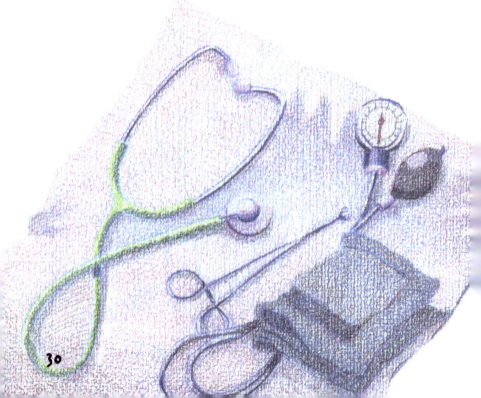

"Doctor, you know what? I've made up my mind. I'm going to have this baby. Will you help me? Can I call you at night if I have to?"

"Of course you can." — Dr Martin answered with a smile. "I'll be by your side at all times. You are not sick, just pregnant. We must be happy for this new life you are expecting. Let's move into the examination room."

When they returned to the office, Barbara was feeling better. She was still a little queasy, but Dr Martin assured her this sensation would soon pass. "Would you like to call your mom in so we can talk a little?" — Dr Martin asked.

When they left the doctor's building, Barbara was feeling better than she had done in a long time. She hugged her mother in the parking lot.

"You know what, Mom? I want to have a big ice cream now."

"Me, too. Let's go."

"Can I have another one if I'm still hungry?"

"Of course you can. I love you, honey."

"I love you too, Mom."

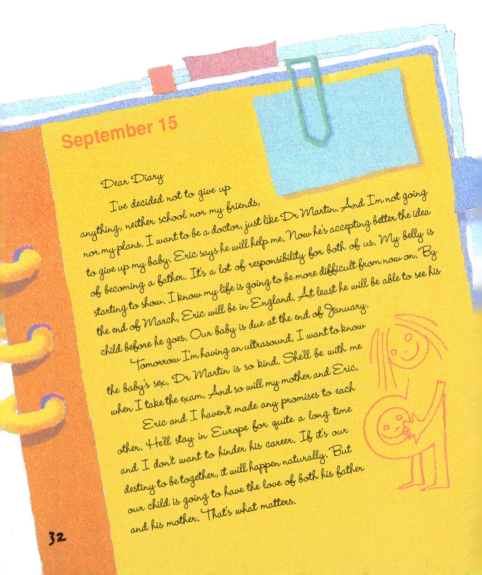

September 15

Dear Diary

I've decided not to give up anything, neither school nor my friends, nor my plans. I want to be a doctor, just like Dr Martin. And I'm not going to give up my baby. Eric says he will help me. Now he's accepting better the idea of becoming a father. It's a lot of responsibility for both of us. My belly is starting to show. I know my life is going to be more difficult from now on. By the end of March, Eric will be in England. At least he will be able to see his child before he goes. Our baby is due at the end of January.

Tomorrow I'm having an ultrasound. I want to know the baby's sex. Dr Martin is so kind. She'll be with me when I take the exam. And so will my mother and Eric.

Eric and I haven't made any promises to each other. He'll stay in Europe for quite a long time and I don't want to hinder his career. If it's our destiny to be together, it will happen naturally. But our child is going to have the love of both his father and his mother. That's what matters.

In the morning, at the lab, Barbara lay down for the ultrasound exam. The doctor spread some gel on her belly. On the monitor screen, shadows started to form and disappear as the doctor ran a mouse-like device all over her abdomen. The doctor looked at Dr Martin and said with a smile: "Are you seeing what I'm seeing?" — Dr Martin smiled back. "Yes, of course I am. Let's take a look again."

Barbara could see nothing but blurred images. After a while the doctor exclaimed: "Twins! You are expecting two babies! As we can see here, they are in two different placentas, so they are not identical. Let's see if we can see their sex." Barbara was feeling dizzy. Her mother and Eric were crying. He held her hand really tight. She thought, "Oh, my God, one baby would be hard, imagine two!"

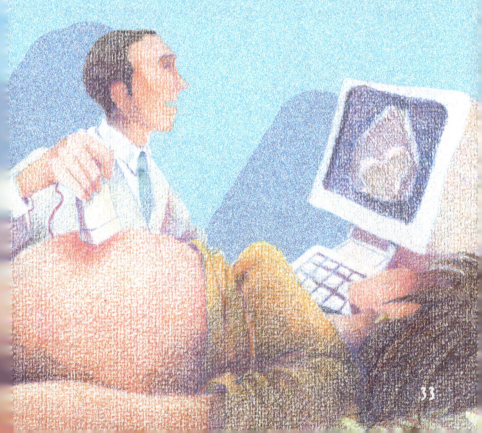

Ten years later...

I had the permission of the girls and of all the people involved in this story to write it. I myself know better than anyone what Barbara has gone through during these past ten years — laughter and tears all mixed together. Babs, that insecure teenager who didn't want to lose her first boyfriend, was me.

I didn't become a doctor as I had planned. I graduated in Biology instead. I'm a teacher now. Eric got his master's degree and came back home after three years. He and I didn't get married but we are still best friends. He's a loving father to our two girls. I met a wonderful person last year. He's also a Biology teacher. We're thinking about getting married soon. We both do volunteer work for an NGO which helps teenagers in risky situations. We organize workshops and camping trips with groups of students from public schools to alert them to the risks of early pregnancy and Sexually Transmitted Diseases, such as Aids.

At these meetings, we don't really <u>teach</u>. We try to create a friendly environment in which they can talk about their doubts, feelings and fears. During these discussions, we try to pass on valuable information which can enable them to make the best decisions at the right time. I share my story with them and I also say that prevention is the responsible thing to do.

In our workshops and on our camping trips, we also provide the teenagers with some technical data.

According to the United Nations:

- the world has today the highest rate of youngsters from 10 to 19 years of age in history: 1.2 billion pre-teens and teens;

- Brazil has 52 million adolescents; 87% of the world's young population lives in underdeveloped countries;

- 462 million youngsters survive with less than US$ 2 per day and 238 million live with an income lower than US$ 1 a day;

- over 13 million children have become orphans due to their parents' deaths from AIDS. The forecast is that this number will double by the year 2010;

- one teenager is infected by AIDS every 14 seconds. Almost half of the new cases affect the world's young population;

- 14 million girls get pregnant every year and pregnancy has been on the rise among girls between 10 and 12 years of age;
- 57 million young men in underdeveloped countries are illiterate; the number of young women in the same situation has risen to 96 million;
- Brazil occupies the third position in Latin America in the ranking of girls' deaths during delivery: 277 deaths for every one thousand pregnant girls.

These are dire statistics. All of us must do our part to change this terrible situation: parents, teachers, the community, NGO's and governments.

Oh, I almost forgot to say that during those difficult times in my life, I could count on my supportive web friends, amongst other people. Their friendship is one of the things I treasure the most. Among my dearest memories of that period is the double baby shower they prepared for me. It was just wonderful!

KEY WORDS

The meaning of each word corresponds to its use in the context of the story (see page number 00)

abroad (27) fora do país, no exterior
actually (3) na verdade
advice (7) conselho
apologize (25) desculpar-se
avoid (9) evitar
aware of (14) estar consciente de
baby shower (36) chá de bebê
belly (29) barriga
blame (23) culpar
blurred (33) borrado(a), indistinto(a)
break up, broke up, broken up (6) romper (namoro, por exemplo)
careless (17) descuidado(a)
complain, complains (5) reclamar
condom (9) preservativo masculino, "camisinha"
data (35) dados, informações
delivery (36) parto
deserve (5) merecer
device (33) aparelho
dire (36) terrível, sombrio(a)
dizzy (33) tonto(a), com tontura
due (32) em uma certa data
duty (30) dever, obrigação
enable (35) capacitar, tornar capaz
fake (8) inventar
forecast (35) previsão
give a shot (20) tentar
give in, gave in (17) ceder
give up, gave up, given up (6) desistir
guilty (17) culpado(a)
hinder (32) atrapalhar
hug (19) abraço

illiterate (36) analfabeto(a)
in regards to (9) com relação a
income (35) renda
intercourse (9) relação sexual
issue (9) assunto, tema
let down (21) desapontar
make up one's mind (31) decidir-se
melt away (30) desaparecer, desfazer-se
mess up (22) entrar numa situação difícil
on the rise (36) estar aumentando
otherwise (30) caso contrário
pregnancy (9) gravidez
queasy (31) enjoado(a)
quit (26) desistir, abandonar
rate (35) taxa
scholarship (27) bolsa de estudos
shadow (33) sombra
share (4) partilhar
should (11) deveria (aconselhamento)
shrink (8) psicoterapeuta (psiquiatra, psicólogo)
shy (3) tímido (a)
to split, split, split (12) romper, separar-se
stare (29) encarar, olhar fixamente
steady (4) estável, constante
throw up, threw up, thrown up (28) vomitar
twins (33) gêmeos
used to (3) costumava(m)
valuable (35) importante, valioso(a)
wonder (13) pensar, imaginar

ACTIVITIES

Before Reading

1. Take a piece of paper. Write down your main doubt in relation to sexuality and /or STD'S (Sexually Transmitted Diseases). Don't sign your name. Fold the piece of paper.

While Reading

2. Who said these things in the story? Write the names of the characters.

   a) __Barbara__ I love him! I love him! I love him!

   b) _____ We deserve a little fun, don't we?

   c) _____ Who can please parents?

   c) _____ I'm going to dream about Eric, the one and only.

   d) _____ I feel like an adult and so does he.

3. Who does/did these things in the story? Write the names.

   a) _____ **She** wrote Dr Devane a letter.

   b) _____ **She** kept a diary.

   c) _____ **He** tried to comfort his friend.

   d) _____ **She** asked questions and examined Barbara.

   e) _____ **They** organize workshops and camping trips.

4. Use the prepositions from the box to form phrasal verbs. You can use the same preposition more than once if necessary. There are more prepositions than you need.

   > up in for on at from out to about through

   a) Barbara hasn't given _____ school.

   b) She and her boyfriend broke _____ last week.

   c) If you are looking _____ advice, you can write to that magazine.

d) Could you please fill _____ this questionnaire?

e) She couldn't call her friends _____. She didn't have their numbers.

f) He insisted and she finally gave _____.

g) I can't make _____ my mind!

h) She has gone _____ some difficult times.

5. Write words which have the same meaning. All the words are in the story. Another important word will be formed with the first letter of each of these words.

a) meet a boyfriend/girlfriend = _____ (4 letters)

b) everybody = _____ (8 letters)

c) the opposite of **go** = _____ (4 letters)

d) the opposite of **out** = _____ (2 letters)

e) something you can only share with a friend = _____ (6 letters)

f) subject = _____ (5 letters)

g) common = _____ (8 letters)

h) not once = _____ (5 letters)

After Reading

6. Put the pieces of papers with the questions you and your classmates wrote in activity 1 into a box. In turns, take a piece of paper from the box and read the question. Discuss the possible answer(s) with your friends.